AF604605

WOMEN
IN
GREAT
AUSSIE
SPORTS
WOMEN'S
SOCCER
TONY LA TORRACA
REDBACK
publishing

First Published 2025 by
Redback Publishing
Suite 6, 13a Narabang Way,
Belrose NSW 2085
Australia

www.redbackpublishing.com
orders@redbackpublishing.com

ISBN 978-1-761401-15-2 HBK

Author: Tony La Torraca
Editor: Anton Desser
Designer: Redback Publishing

Original illustrations © Redback Publishing 2025
Originated by Redback Publishing

Acknowledgements
Abbreviations: l—left, r—right, b—bottom, t—top, c—centre, m—middle
We would like to thank the following for permission to reproduce photographs: (Images © shutterstock, Alamy)

Pg2-3 IOIO IMAGES / Shutterstock.com, pg4 IOIO IMAGES / Shutterstock.com, pg5 IOIO IMAGES / Shutterstock.com, pg6 IOIO IMAGES / Shutterstock.com, pg7t Federico Guerra Moran / Shutterstock.com, pg7b IOIO IMAGES / Shutterstock.com, pg8t IOIO IMAGES / Shutterstock.com, pg8b IOIO IMAGES / Shutterstock.com, pg9t IOIO IMAGES / Shutterstock.com, pg9b IOIO IMAGES / Shutterstock.com, pg10bc IOIO IMAGES / Shutterstock.com, pg12t Victor Velter / Shutterstock.com, pg13ml FiledIMAGE / Shutterstock.com, pg13bl IOIO IMAGES / Shutterstock.com, pg14tl IOIO IMAGES / Shutterstock.com, pg14tr IOIO IMAGES / Shutterstock.com, pg14bl IOIO IMAGES / Shutterstock.com, pg15tl lev radin / Shutterstock.com, pg15br IOIO IMAGES / Shutterstock.com, pg16tl FiledIMAGE / Shutterstock.com, pg16br IOIO IMAGES / Shutterstock.com, pg18tr Hyserb / Shutterstock.com, pg18bl Federico Guerra Moran / Shutterstock.com, pg191tr Natursports / Shutterstock.com, pg19br Oleksandr Osipov / Shutterstock.com, pg19bl IOIO IMAGES / Shutterstock.com, pg20tl IOIO IMAGES / Shutterstock.com, pg20br IOIO IMAGES / Shutterstock.com, pg21tr IOIO IMAGES / Shutterstock.com, pg20mr blues4ever / Shutterstock.com, pg21br IOIO IMAGES / Shutterstock.com, pg22tl Speed Media / Alamy Stock Photo, pg22br ssi77 / Shutterstock.com, pg22bl SnowStore6789 / Shutterstock.com, pg25tr IOIO IMAGES / Shutterstock.com, pg21br kandschwar, CC BY 3.0 <https://creativecommons.org/licenses/by/3.0>, via Wikimedia Commons, pg26tr Ryan Fletcher / Shutterstock.com, pg27br IOIO IMAGES / Shutterstock.com, pg29bl Speed Media / Alamy Stock Photo.

A catalogue record for this book is available from the National Library of Australia

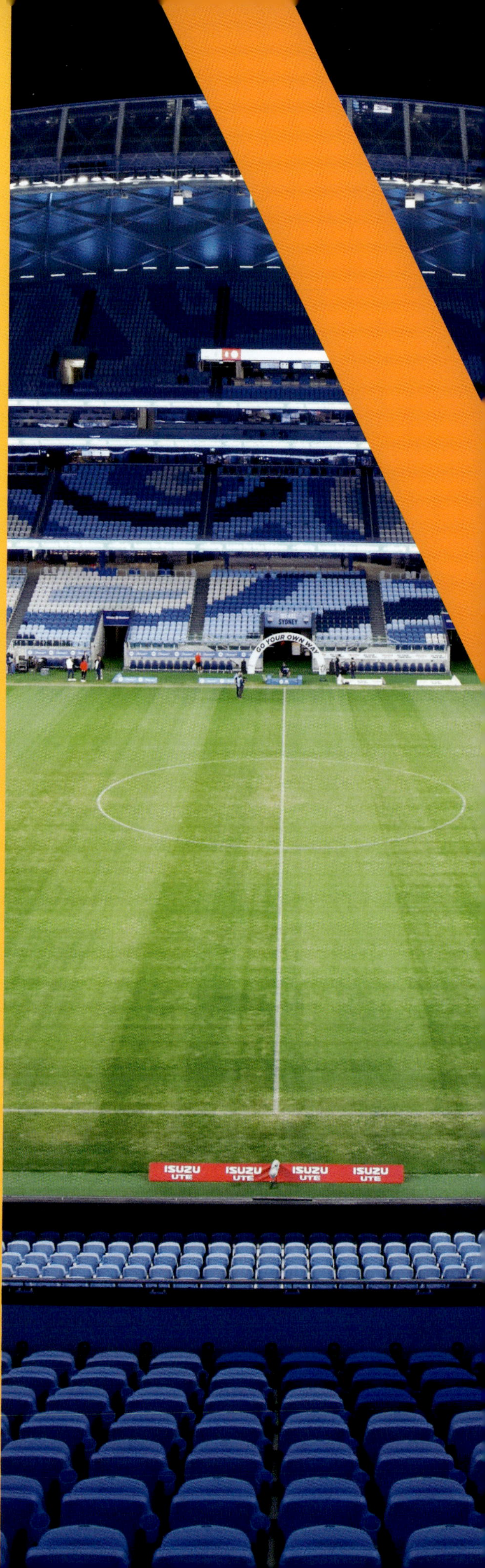

CONTENTS

PLAYER PROFILES

SOCCER IN AUSTRALIA

For over a century, Australians have actively engaged in soccer. The women's national soccer team, known as the Matildas, has gained notable success on the global stage, with their achievements continually on the rise. The growing enthusiasm for soccer is evident in the increased participation of amateurs in local teams and leagues, contributing to the expanding fan base supporting the national team.

Australia's top women's soccer league was the Women's National Soccer League (WNSL), which unfortunately came to an end in 2004. Following this, the W-League emerged with an initial roster of eight teams: Adelaide United, Brisbane Roar, Central Coast Mariners, Melbourne Victory, Newcastle Jets, Perth Glory, Sydney FC, and Canberra United. Notably, seven of these teams were affiliated with A-League clubs. The competition maintained its eight-team format until the 2012-2013 season when the inclusion of the Western Sydney Wonderers expanded the competition to 9 teams.

A-LEAGUE WOMEN

The premier women's association football league in Australia, formerly known as the W-League, has been rebranded as the A-League Women soccer competition. Established in 2008 by Football Australia, the league initially featured eight teams, seven of which were affiliated with existing A-League Men's clubs. As of the 2021–22 season, the competition expanded to include ten teams (with further expansion plans to twelve teams), unified under the A-Leagues banner.

The league's schedule typically spans from November to February and comprises a 22-round regular season. The conclusion of the season involves an end-of-season finals series playoff tournament, where the highest-placed teams compete, ending in a Grand Final match to determine the ultimate champion.

HISTORY

On May 13, 2015, it was confirmed that Melbourne City would join the W-League starting from the 2015–16 season. The club had an outstanding debut season, winning all 12 of its regular-season matches and securing victory in the Grand Final.

Initially governed by Football Federation Australia (FFA) since its inception, the league's operational control underwent a shift in July 2019. The FFA handed over operational control to individual clubs, which were collectively represented by the Australian Professional Football Clubs Association.

In a bid for expansion, Wellington Phoenix was introduced as a new club for the 2021–22 A-League Women season. Further expansion was announced for the 2022–23 season, with Western United joining the league and Central Coast Mariners to rejoin for the 2023-24 season, thereby increasing the total number of teams to 12.

Since its inaugural season in 2008, a total of 12 clubs have participated in the A-League Women competition, showcasing the evolving landscape and growth of women's soccer in Australia.

CLUB	CITY	YEARS ACTIVE
Adelaide United	Adelaide	2008-current
Brisbane Roar (Queensland Roar)	Brisbane	2008-current
Canberra United	Canberra	2008-current
Central Coast United	Gosford	2008-2009
Melbourne City	Melbourne	2015-current
Melbourne Victory	Melbourne	2008-current
Newcastle Jets	Newcastle	2008-current
Perth Glory	Perth	2008-current
Sydney FC	Sydney	2008-current
Wellington Phoenix	Wellington	2021-current
Western Sydney	Sydney	2012-current
Western United	Sydney	2022-current

EXCITING SKILLS

What are the 6 basic soccer skills?

Soccer is frequently referred to as "the beautiful game," yet to play it with grace, one must first master the fundamental skills of the sport.

Basic soccer skills:

- Passing
- Dribbling
- Trapping / receiving the ball
- Heading the ball
- Shooting the ball
- Movement off the ball ** (Bonus skill)

Soccer is frequently used as a tool to instill teamwork, competition, and the essential elements of a healthy, active lifestyle in young children. While this serves as a solid beginning, the earlier children grasp the correct techniques of the game, the stronger their groundwork will be for a sustained soccer journey.

PLAYER PROFILE

SAM KERR

Sam Kerr was born in Western Australia. At the age of 12, she was introduced to soccer by her family. Three years later, she made her debut for the Australian women's national soccer team.

Kerr joined Chelsea Football Club on a two-and-a-half-year deal during the second half of the 2019/20 Barclays Women's Super League season. She later extended her contract, committing to the club until 2024.

Internationally recognised as a football superstar, Kerr made her debut for Australia at the age of 15 and notably scored five goals at the 2019 World Cup.

In 2023, during the World Cup hosted by Australia and New Zealand, Kerr unfortunately missed the group stage due to injury but made a comeback in the last match against Denmark. She scored in a semi-final defeat to England, and her goal earned a nomination for FIFA's Puskas Award for the best goal in world football in 2023.

Kerr missed the Paris Olympics due to injury.

FUNDAMENTALS

In football, the ultimate objective is to win by scoring goals, and shooting is the key to achieving this. Without attempts on goal, you cannot win. Success in soccer hinges on mastering not only the power of your shots but also the crucial elements of control and accuracy.

For beginners in soccer, it is important to commence with the fundamental skill of shooting. Beyond sheer power, emphasis should be placed on developing control and precision. Recognising that soccer is a team sport, passing emerges as the primary skill. Accurate passing facilitates the seamless transfer of the ball between players, enabling swift movement across the field with minimal effort compared to dribbling.

While dribbling is an individual skill, it is essential to learn that soccer thrives on teamwork. While in possession of the ball it is important to keep awareness of teammates' positions by looking up and scanning the surroundings for effective passing. Equally important for players without possession of the ball is communication – vocalising and indicating their location to teammates is crucial.

There are many techniques for passing a soccer ball, but the most basic is to use the inside of the foot. This method provides players with optimal control and accuracy. Understanding and honing these fundamental skills lay the groundwork for success in soccer, emphasising the significance of both individual abilities and cohesive teamwork.

BASIC SHOOTING TECHNIQUE IN SOCCER

Mastering the skill of receiving or trapping the ball is indispensable in soccer because failing to control the ball promptly may result in losing possession. The ability to receive the ball should be practised in conjunction with passing.

As you approach the ball, start by planting your support (non-kicking) foot next to the ball, positioning your toes toward the goal. Maintain enough distance from the ball to allow for a clean strike with your shooting foot. Keep your focus on the ball, ensure your ankle is locked, and position your knee over the ball.

Subsequently, execute the strike using the laces of your shoe, aiming for the middle of the ball. This technique enhances control and sets the stage for effective ball handling.

PLAYER PROFILE

MARY FOWLER

Mary Fowler was born on February 14, 2003, in Cairns, Queensland.

During her time at Holy Cross School in Cairns, Fowler played junior football for Saints FC and Leichhardt FC in the local league. Remarkably, she was selected to join the Queensland state under-12s team at the age of 10. At 11, Fowler and her family moved to the Netherlands for three years. Returning to Australia at the age of 14, she enrolled in Wollongong High School of the Performing Arts and joined Bankstown City in the NSW Women's National Premier League. At 16, Fowler signed her first professional contract with Adelaide United in 2019.

In January 2020, she made a significant move to French Ligue 1 club Montpellier HSC. In June 2022, she signed a four-year contract with English FA WSL club Manchester City.

Fowler's international career includes being called up to the Australian squad for the 2019 FIFA Women's World Cup and being selected for the 2020 Summer Olympics. She was also part of the Matildas squad for the 2023 FIFA Women's World Cup, where she played a pivotal role in the absence of squad captain Sam Kerr. She played for the Matildas in the 2024 Paris Olympics.

DURATION OF THE GAME

Soccer games consist of two halves, each lasting 45 minutes, with a maximum 15-minute break permitted between them. The referee has the authority to add extra time at the conclusion of each half to compensate for any time lost due to stoppages.

At the elite level, if the scores remain tied after the referee signals the end of the match, extra time is introduced. This additional period typically spans 15 minutes, divided into two segments of seven-and-a-half minutes each. The referee may also include stoppage time within the 15 minutes of extra time to account for any interruptions. This ensures a fair and comprehensive resolution in high-level soccer matches.

PLAYER POSITIONS

In soccer, there are three primary position areas on the field, in addition to the goalkeeper:

DEFENCE

Defenders typically operate in the defensive half of the pitch, but it's not uncommon for them to advance into the attacking zone when needed. Fullbacks, positioned near the goalkeeper, provide additional defensive support.

MIDFIELD

Midfielders have a dynamic role, transitioning between defensive and offensive play based on the game's developments. Their crucial responsibility involves bridging the gap between the defensive and attacking units, facilitating smooth transitions.

FORWARD

(ATTACKING ZONE)

Forwards, situated in the attacking zone, encompass specialised strikers or goal scorers. They receive passes from midfielders and play a pivotal role in launching attacks on the opponent's goal.

Players are not strictly confined to their designated positions. Defenders, for instance, may venture into the attacking zone, and midfielders adapt their positions based on the flow of the game. This flexibility allows teams to strategically adjust their formations and tactics as needed.

PLAYER PROFILE

ELLIE MADISON CARPENTER

Ellie Madison Carpenter was born on April 28, 2000.

Carpenter achieved a significant milestone by making her debut for the Australia national team at the age of 15, becoming the first international soccer player – male or female – born in the 21st century to represent the country. Additionally, she holds the distinction of being the youngest Australian participant at the Rio 2016 Olympic Games and the youngest female footballer ever to compete in Olympic history. Her W-League debut also occurred at the age of 15, and in May 2018, she became the youngest player in NWSL history to appear in a game at the age of 18.

She was raised in Cowra, New South Wales. At the age of 12, her family relocated to Sydney.

Carpenter's club journey includes playing for Western Sydney Wanderers FC (2015–2016), Canberra United FC (2017–2018), and Portland Thorns (2018–2020). During the 2019–2020 season, she joined Melbourne City FC on a one-season loan.

In June 2020, Carpenter made a move to Lyon. Representing Australia for the Matildas since 2015, Carpenter made her World Cup debut at the 2019 FIFA Women's World Cup in France at the age of 19. She was also part of the Matildas' Tokyo 2020 Olympics squad and was selected for the 2023 FIFA Women's World Cup. She played for the Matildas in the 2024 Paris Olympics.

PLAYERS AND SUBSTITUTION

Each team is allowed to have a maximum of 11 players on the field simultaneously, with one designated as the goalkeeper. The remaining team members wait on the bench until needed to substitute an injured, fatigued, or underperforming player. In competitions organised by FIFA, a maximum of three substitutions can be made during a match. However, in other matches, teams have the flexibility to make up to five substitutions. Once substituted, a player cannot rejoin the match, and substitutes cannot replace a player who has been sent off by the referee. In such cases, the team must continue playing with a reduced number of players as a consequence of the penalty.

MAKING SUBSTITUTIONS

Team managers or coaches are responsible for initiating substitutions in a soccer match, and they must inform the referee before making a change. The substitute is only allowed to enter the field once the player being replaced has exited via the nearest touchline. In significant matches, such as international games, a game official typically displays the numbers of both the substituted player and the substituting player, making it clear for everyone involved.

PLAYER PROFILE

HAYLEY EMMA RASO

Hayley Emma Raso was born on September 5, 1994. Growing up on the Gold Coast, she played junior football for Palm Beach and attended Emmanuel College during her schooling.

Raso commenced her senior career with Canberra United in 2011 before making her mark in the Women's Super League. Following her release by Everton on August 17, 2021, she joined Manchester City.

Representing the Australian women's national soccer team, the Matildas, since 2012, Raso has been a part of significant tournaments, including the 2019 FIFA Women's World Cup and the 2020 Summer Olympics. She previously played for the under-20 national team, the Young Matildas.

On July 3, 2023, Raso was selected in the Matildas squad for the 2023 FIFA Women's World Cup. She played for the Matildas in the 2024 Paris Olympics.

STARTS AND RESTARTS

Key points regarding starting or restarting a soccer game include:

- Before the game begins, the referee conducts a coin toss. The captain winning the toss decides which goal to attack in the first half and which team takes the kick-off. At the start of the second half, the teams switch ends of the pitch.
- Following a goal, play resumes from the centre of the pitch.
- During the initiation or restart of play, all players must be positioned in their respective halves of the field.
- Once the kick-off is executed, players have the freedom to move into their opponent's half, provided they adhere to the offside rule.

THE CORNER KICK

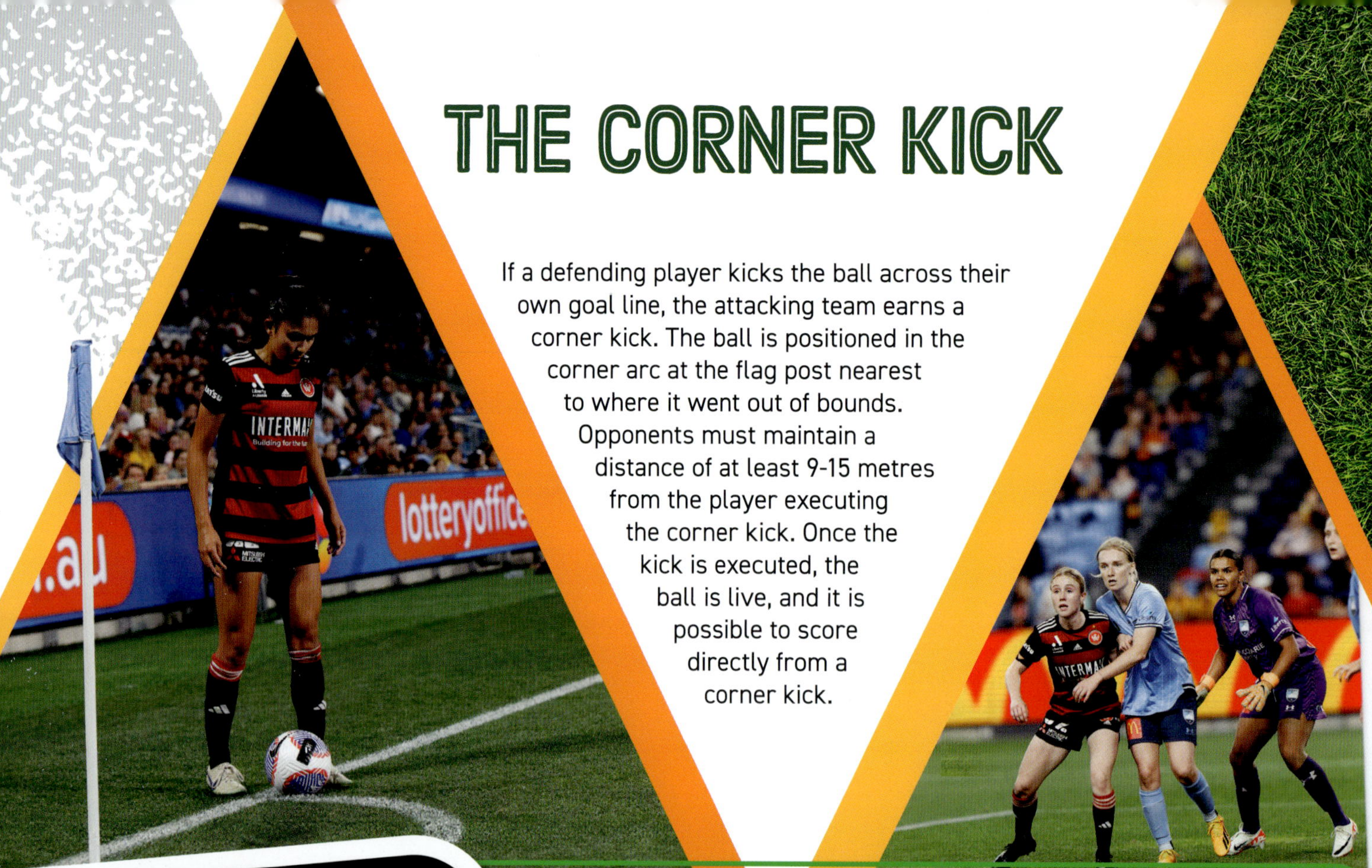

If a defending player kicks the ball across their own goal line, the attacking team earns a corner kick. The ball is positioned in the corner arc at the flag post nearest to where it went out of bounds. Opponents must maintain a distance of at least 9-15 metres from the player executing the corner kick. Once the kick is executed, the ball is live, and it is possible to score directly from a corner kick.

PLAYER PROFILE

CAITLIN JADE FOORD

Caitlin Jade Foord was born on November 11, 1994, and was appointed as a forward for the FA Women's Super League club Arsenal and the Australia national team, the Matildas. Notably, she holds the distinction of being the youngest Australian to participate in a World Cup, representing Australia at the 2011 FIFA Women's World Cup at the age of 16.

Raised in Shellharbour, New South Wales, Foord attended Illawarra Sports High School. In January 24, 2020, Foord left Sydney FC to join the FA WSL club Arsenal.

She made her debut for the Matildas at the age of 16 and has been a consistent presence since 2011.

Foord continued to contribute to the national team's success. She played a crucial role in the Matildas' qualification for the Tokyo 2020 Olympics.

In the 2023 FIFA Women's World Cup, during the Round of 16 against Denmark, Foord scored the opening goal in a 2-0 victory. She played for the Matildas in the 2024 Paris Olympics.

THE GOAL KICK

A goal kick is used to resume play when a player from the attacking team kicks the ball over the goal line, but not between the goal posts. While any player from the defending team has the option to take the goal kick, it is typically the goalkeeper who assumes this responsibility. The kick must originate from the goal area and is promptly considered back in play. In 2019, rules were amended to prevent intentional time-wasting, modifying the requirement for how far the ball needed to travel before being deemed back in play. Before this change, the ball had to cross the penalty line.

THE THROW-IN

If the ball crosses the sideline due to a player's body or foot contact, the opposing team receives a throw-in at the spot where the ball exited the field. The player granted the throw-in positions herself along the touchline, facing the field, and raises the ball above her head. Subsequently, she throws the ball back into play to a teammate. It's important to note that goals cannot be scored directly from a throw-in.

PLAYER PROFILE

STEPHANIE-ELISE CATLEY

Stephanie-Elise Catley was born on January 26, 1994, and was appointed as a defender for Arsenal and the Australia national team. Hailing from Melbourne, Catley embarked on her soccer journey at the age of six. At 13, she became a part of Sandringham, one of Victoria's prominent soccer clubs, and by the age of 15, Catley earned a spot on the under-17 national team after making her first state team.

At 21, Catley competed in the 2015 FIFA Women's World Cup in Canada with the Matildas. She continued to represent Australia in subsequent events such as the 2017 Algarve Cup and the 2017 Tournament of Nations.

Recognising her leadership qualities, Catley was appointed vice-captain for the Matildas squad for the 2019 FIFA Women's World Cup in France on May 14, 2019. She maintained her role as vice-captain for the Matildas in the Tokyo 2020 Olympics.

In 2023, Catley resumed her role as vice-captain for the Matildas in the 2023 FIFA Women's World Cup. She played for the Matildas in the 2024 Paris Olympics.

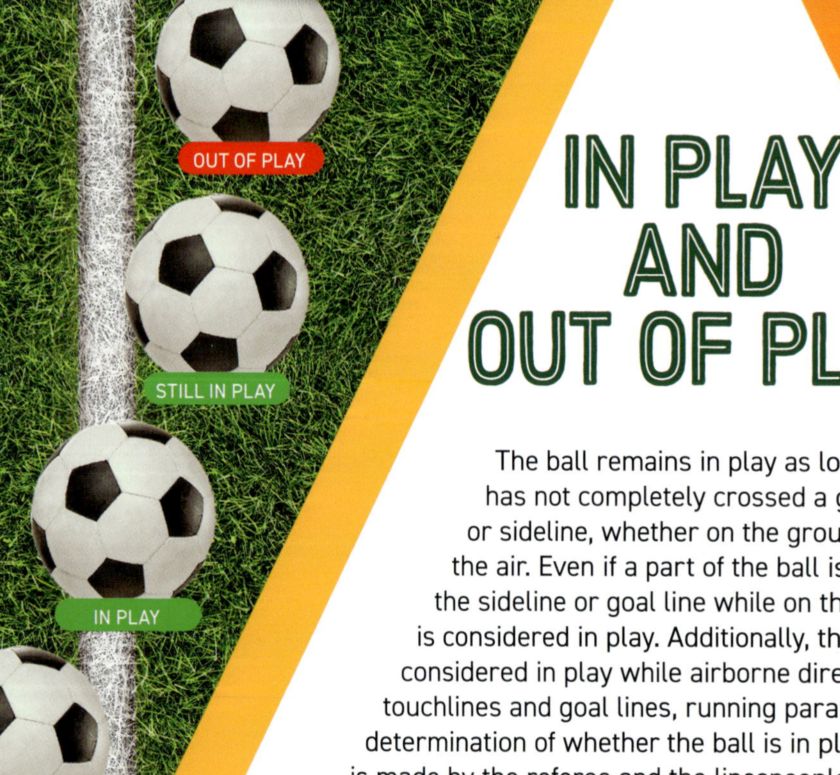

IN PLAY AND OUT OF PLAY

The ball remains in play as long as it has not completely crossed a goal line or sideline, whether on the ground or in the air. Even if a part of the ball is touching the sideline or goal line while on the ground, it is considered in play. Additionally, the ball is still considered in play while airborne directly above the touchlines and goal lines, running parallel to them. The determination of whether the ball is in play or out of play is made by the referee and the linespeople.

THE OFFSIDE RULE

Being in an offside position is considered an offence if it puts the opposing team at a disadvantage. A player is deemed offside when she is on her team's attacking half of the pitch and closer to the ball than all opponents, excluding the goalkeeper. This rule is implemented to prevent players from advancing ahead of the ball and opponents before it is played, as such actions limit the ability of opponents to compete for possession.

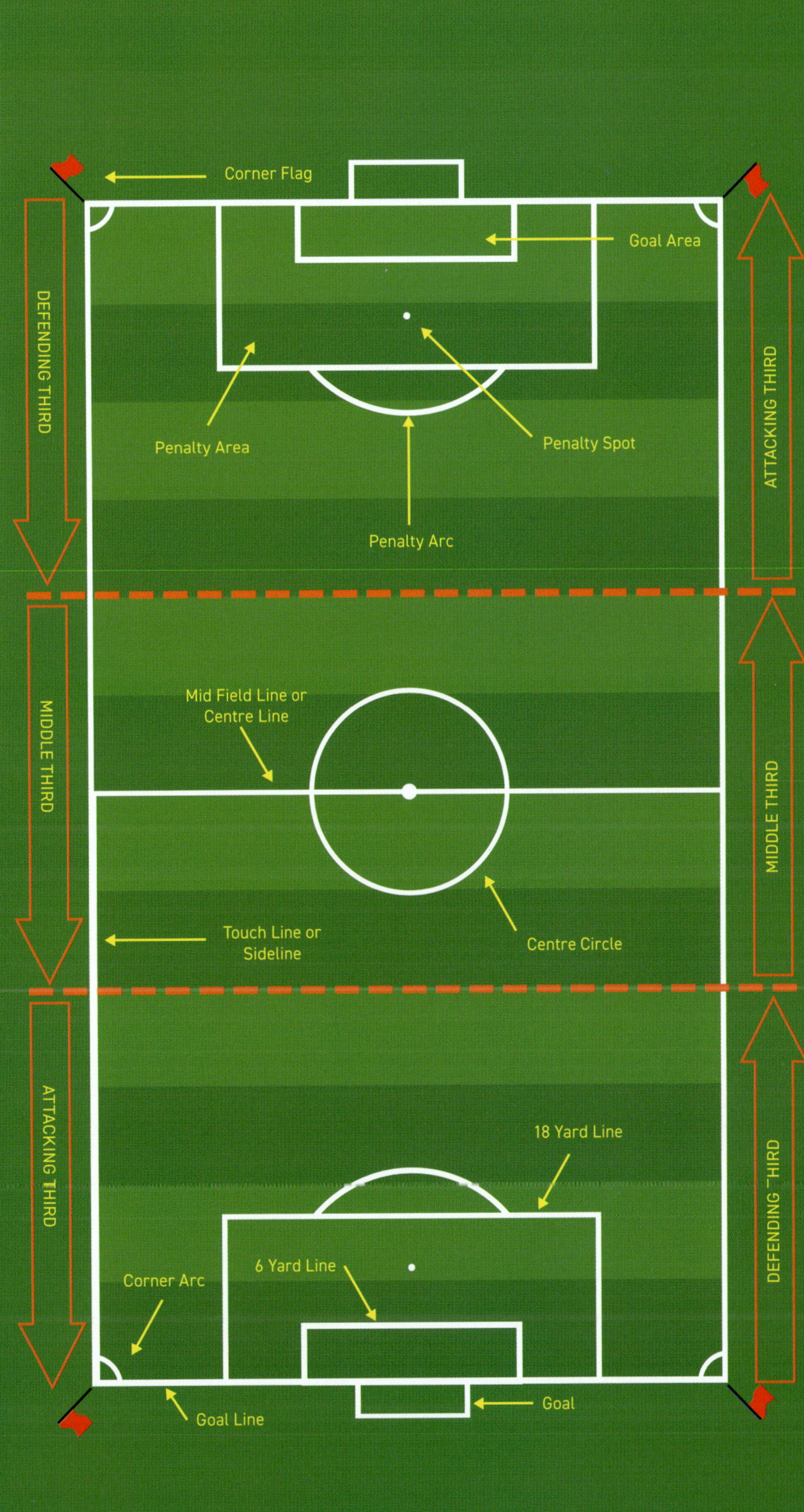

THE LINESPEOPLE OR ASSISTANTS

The assistant referees, also known as linespeople, closely monitor the game to ensure that when the ball is played from one half of the pitch to the other, attacking players haven't initiated their forward run too early. If an offside violation is detected by a linesperson or assistant referee, she raises a flag, prompting the referee to blow the whistle. Subsequently, possession is given to a player on the opposing team. It's worth noting that a player is not considered offside if she receives the ball directly from a goal kick, a throw-in, or a corner kick. Offside calls often require quick judgment, and errors may occur.

PLAYER PROFILE

ALANNA KENNEDY

Alanna Kennedy was born on January 21, 1995, and she was appointed as a defender for Manchester City in the English FA Women's Super League. While primarily known as a centre back on the international stage, she also possesses the ability to play in the midfielder position.

Her W-League journey began with Sydney FC in the 2010–11 season, and she later played for Newcastle Jets in the 2011–12 season. After a stint with Western Sydney Wanderers in the 2013–14 season and Perth Glory in the 2014 season, Kennedy returned to Sydney FC in 2015.

Kennedy's international career includes being named in the Matildas squad for the 2019 FIFA Women's World Cup, where she also represented the Matildas in the Tokyo 2020 Olympics squad. Additionally, she was part of the Matildas' roster for the 2023 FIFA Women's World Cup. She played for the Matildas in the 2024 Paris Olympics.

THE BALL

Guidelines dictate the dimensions, weight and shape of the soccer ball utilised in an official match. The referee examines the ball at the beginning of each half to ensure it adheres to these specifications:

- The ball must be spherical (round) and crafted from leather or a comparable material.
- Its circumference should fall within the range of 68 to 70 centimetres.
- The weight of the ball must range from 410 to 450 grams.
- The ball must be inflated to a pressure of 600-1100 grams per square centimetre.

PENALTIES AND INFRINGEMENTS

When a player violates the rules, it is referred to as committing a "foul." It is the responsibility of the referee to determine if any player has breached the rules by acting in a careless, reckless, or excessively forceful manner.

RED AND YELLOW CARDS

When a player commits a serious offence that merits a caution, the referee addresses the offending player and shows a yellow warning card. Additionally, the referee has the authority to present a red card to a player, either instantly or after the player has already received a yellow warning card. If a player is shown a red card, immediate departure from the field is required, and no substitution is allowed.

PENALTY KICKS

If a player commits an offence resulting in a free kick within her own penalty area, the opposing team may be awarded a penalty kick. This kick is executed from the penalty spot, located inside the penalty area. During a penalty kick, all players on the field, excluding the goalkeeper and the player taking the penalty, must remain outside the penalty area and at a distance of at least 9-15 metres behind the penalty spot. The penalty kick involves a direct contest between the goalkeeper of one team and a player from the attacking team. The player taking the penalty kick aims to kick the ball past the goalkeeper and into the net. The goalkeeper is required to have at least one foot on the goal line as the ball is kicked, before attempting to prevent the ball from entering the goal.

FREE KICKS

Offences that could result in a free kick being granted against a player include:

- Kicking or trying to kick an opponent.
- Tripping an opponent.
- Charging or pushing an opponent.
- Tackling an opponent with the intention of gaining possession but making contact with the opponent before the ball.
- Holding an opponent.
- Deliberately handling the ball (excluding the goalkeeper).
- Playing in a manner considered dangerous.
- Preventing an opponent from moving.

Mackenzie Elizabeth Arnold was born on February 25, 1994. She became goalkeeper and captain for the Women's Super League club West Ham, and joined the Australia national team. Arnold was born on the Gold Coast and initiated her junior football career with Burleigh Heads.

Her professional journey began in 2012 when she joined Canberra United from Perth Glory for the 2012–13 W-League season.

She was part of the Matildas squad for the 2015 World Cup in Canada, the 2016 Summer Olympics, and the 2019 World Cup in France. Arnold continued her role as a goalkeeper for the Matildas in the Tokyo 2020 Olympics. Additionally, she was a vital member of the Matildas' 2023 FIFA Women's World Cup squad, contributing her goalkeeping skills for Australia. She played for the Matildas in the 2024 Paris Olympics.

PLAYER PROFILE

MACKENZIE ELIZABETH ARNOLD

NATIONAL TEAMS

The Matildas are Australia's senior women's national soccer team, and they are also the Australian women's Olympic team. They boast a significant history, participating in nine World Cups and two Olympics.

The 2023 FIFA Women's World Cup marked the ninth edition of this quadrennial international women's football championship. Organised by FIFA, the tournament occurred from July 20 to August 20, 2023, and was jointly hosted by Australia and New Zealand. Notably, it was the first Women's World Cup with more than one host nation and the inaugural tournament of its kind held in the Southern Hemisphere.

PLAYER PROFILE

EMILY VAN EGMOND

Emily Van Egmond was born on July 12, 1993.

Hailing from Newcastle, Australia, van Egmond embarked on her football journey at the age of five. She is the daughter of Gary van Egmond, a former Socceroo and coach for Newcastle United Jets in the A-League.

Van Egmond initially represented the Young Matildas at the under-20 level. Her inclusion in the Australia national team came in 2010, leading to her participation in the 2011 World Cup held in Germany. She continued to contribute to the Matildas and was selected for the Tokyo 2020 Olympics.

On July 3, 2023, she was nominated for the World Cup in her home country. She played for the Matildas in the 2024 Paris Olympics.

DID YOU KNOW?

The Australian senior women's football team, the Matildas, were the first ever Aussies to compete in soccer at the Olympic Games.

They Played Canada two days before the opening ceremony in San Paolo.

WOMEN'S WORLD CUP

Thirty-two teams played in the 2023 Women's World Cup, including Australia and New Zealand as the host nations.

Sixty-four games were played over 30 days.

The tournament was spread over multiple host cities and stadiums in each country.

The opening game was played at Eden Park in Auckland and the final match at Stadium Australia Sydney.

GROUP TOURNAMENT

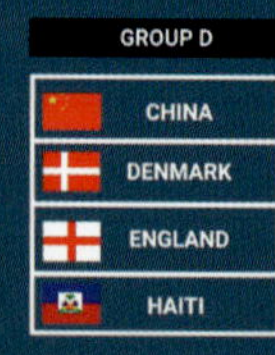

GROUP A	GROUP B	GROUP C	GROUP D
NEW ZEALAND	AUSTRALIA	COSTA RICA	CHINA
NORWAY	CANADA	JAPAN	DENMARK
PHILIPPINES	NIGERIA	SPAIN	ENGLAND
SWITZERLAND	IRELAND	ZAMBIA	HAITI

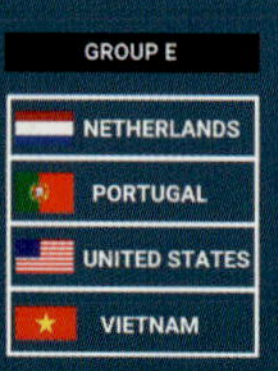

GROUP E	GROUP F	GROUP G	GROUP H
NETHERLANDS	BRAZIL	ARGENTINA	COLOMBIA
PORTUGAL	FRANCE	ITALY	GERMANY
UNITED STATES	JAMAICA	SOUTH AFRICA	SOUTH KOREA
VIETNAM	PANAMA	SWEDEN	MOROCCO

SOCCER FIELD DIMENSIONS

Soccer fields are generally larger than those of other major sports like American Football, but the size of a soccer field can vary based on factors such as the governing body of the league, the age of the players, the number of players, and unique characteristics of each field. Notably, even top governing bodies like FIFA and IFAB provide measurement ranges for length and width rather than specific dimensions.

This variability is a key aspect contributing to the distinctive nature of a home-field advantage in soccer.

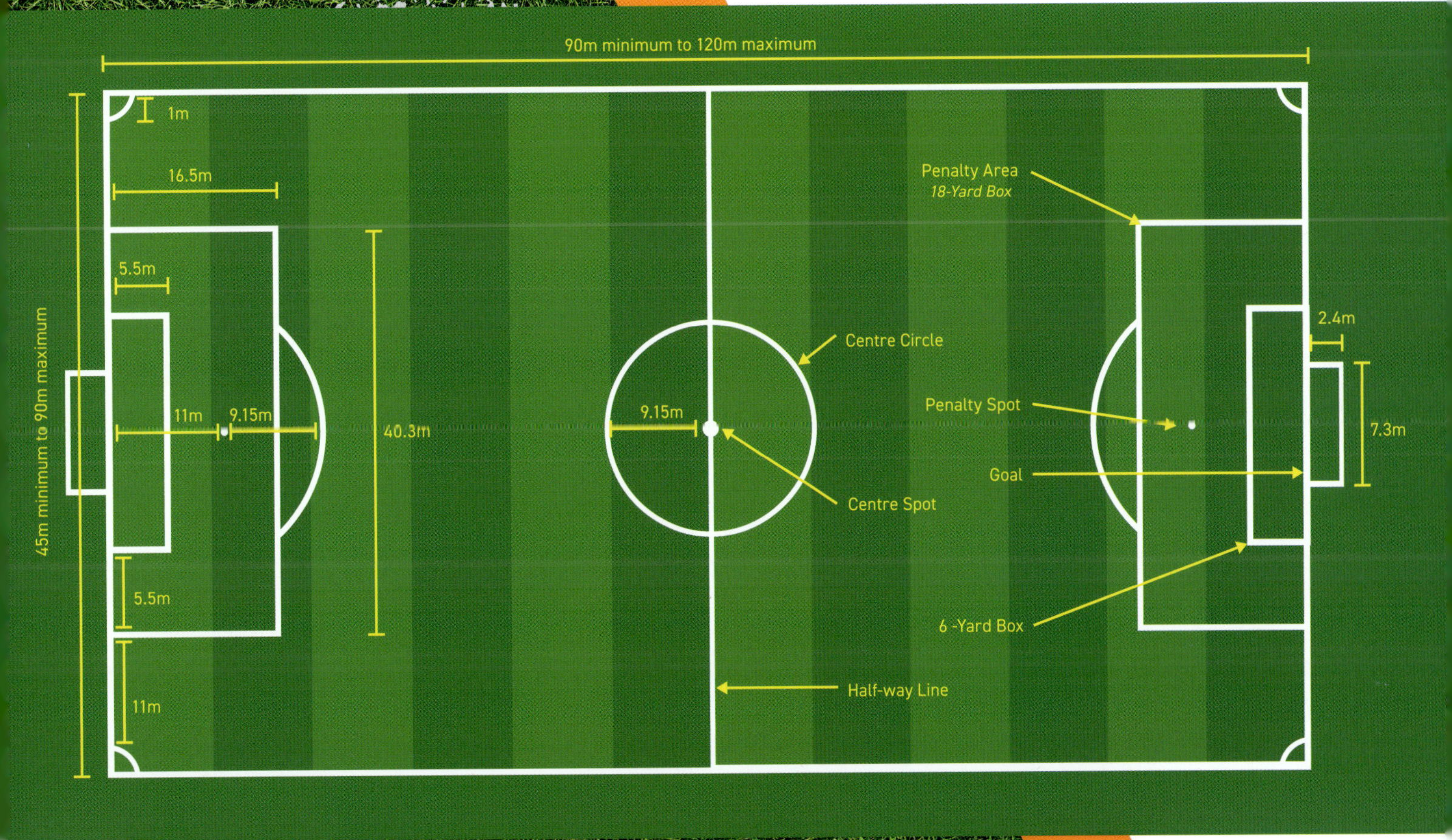

90m minimum to 120m maximum
45m minimum to 90m maximum
1m
16.5m
5.5m
11m
9.15m
40.3m
5.5m
11m
9.15m
Penalty Area
18-Yard Box
Centre Circle
Penalty Spot
Goal
Centre Spot
6 -Yard Box
Half-way Line
2.4m
7.3m

ON FIELD POSITIONS

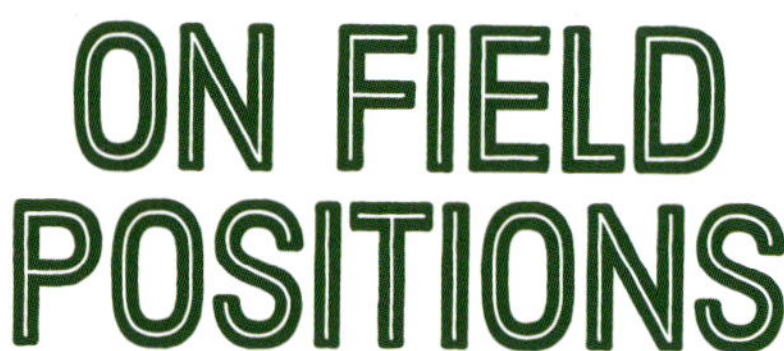

PLAYER POSITIONS

A coach can change the teams formation as part of their strategy, the only position that is mandatory is the goalkeeper.

- Goalkeeper
- The Back Line – Defender positions (Centre-back, sweeper, full-back, left-back and right-back)
- The Midfield – Centre-mid, left-mid and right-mid
- The Forward Line – Attackers – Centre forward/ striker, left winger and right winger

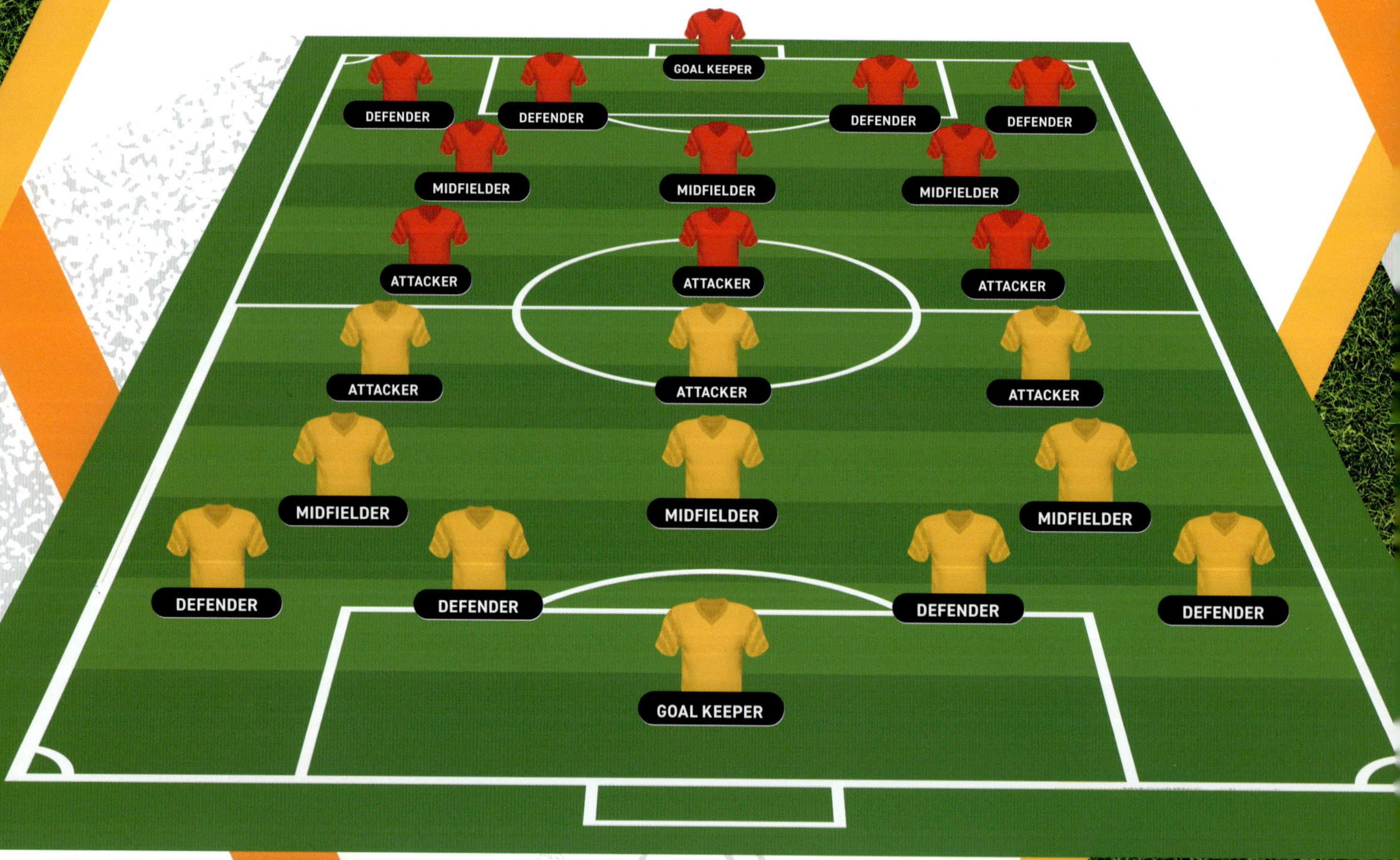

Katrina-Lee Gorry was born on August 13, 1992.

Gorry's early football experience includes playing youth football for Mount Gravatt between 2009 and 2012.

In 2017, Gorry achieved a milestone by becoming the first Roar member to secure a multi-year contract, committing to a two-year deal with Brisbane.

The year 2016 marked Gorry's debut at the Olympics, and she continued to contribute to the Matildas' successes. Gorry played a crucial role in the squad's victory at the 2017 Tournament of Nations. In 2018, she participated in the AFC Women's Asian Cup.

Gorry continued her international journey, competing in the 2020 Olympic Games and making an appearance in the 2023 FIFA Women's World Cup. She played for the Matildas in the 2024 Paris Olympics.

THE YOUNG MATILDAS (UNDER 20s)

The women's under-20s soccer team of Australia participates in international youth tournaments. The Young Matildas made their debut in the inaugural Under-20 Women's World Youth Championship in Canada in 2002, securing a fifth-place finish and marking the first time an Australian soccer team reached the finals of a FIFA world tournament. In 2018, Football Australia introduced the Future Matildas program, aiming to develop and advance female players aged between 15 and 19.

TOURING MATILDAS

The Matildas began their international journey in 1979. Initially, their matches were exclusively against New Zealand until 1986 when they faced China. In 2016, the Matildas reached the quarterfinals at the Rio Olympics but were defeated by Brazil in a penalty shoot-out. This marked the first time in 12 years that an Australian soccer team, in this case the Matildas, had qualified for the Olympic Games.

THE FUTURE MATILDAS

The Future Matildas program was established in 2018 to provide specialised training for some of Australia's most talented 15 to 20-year-old female footballers. The Australian Sports Commission helped fund the program to ensure the senior team has a strong future.

SOCIAL MEDIA

A soccer player's online presence on social media plays a crucial role in their career. A substantial following can lead to lucrative sponsorship deals with various companies leveraging the player's popularity and fan base for their advertising. Social media has rapidly evolved into a significant advertising platform, offering substantial revenue opportunities for influential figures in the sporting world.

MATCH DAY

The game day begins with a light jogging session followed by a matchday program conducted by the fitness staff. This program is tailored to energise the players without exerting them excessively. The top player is then prepared to step onto the field and give their maximum effort.

YOU ARE WHAT YOU EAT

All sports people pay special attention to their diet. A top player requires a diet that builds stamina, and dietitians will work out a menu for each player. All the major food groups are represented in the diet program, with a variation towards match day when carbohydrates are increased to provide the extra energy required.

Cortnee Vine was born on April 9, 1998.

She comes from Shepparton, Victoria, Australia. Her football journey began at the age of five, and by the age of 12 she had secured a spot at the Queensland Academy of Sport.

Representing Australia at both the under-17 and under-20 levels, Vine made her senior team debut in January 2022 against the Philippines at the 2022 AFC Women's Asian Cup.

In July 2023, Vine was named in the Matildas squad for the 2023 FIFA Women's World Cup. Notably, in August 2023, she played a pivotal role by scoring the winning penalty kick in a 7-6 shootout victory over France. She played for the Matildas in the 2024 Paris Olympics.

PLAYER PROFILE

CORTNEE VINE

MEDIA COVERAGE

Australian matches are shown on online subscription streaming services and free-to-air broadcasts. During the Tokyo 2020 Olympics in 2021, the Matildas set TV viewing records for any women's team sport.

Their second group stage match against Sweden drew 1,468,000 viewers, breaking the initial record. The quarter-final against Great Britain then surpassed this with 2.27 million viewers, and the all-time record was established at 2.32 million viewers during the Olympic semi-final against Sweden.

During the 2023 Women's World Cup, the Quarterfinal match between Australia and France achieved an average viewership of over 4 million, peaking at 7.2 million on Channel 7. This became the most-watched sporting event in Australia since Cathy Freeman's 400 metres gold medal win at the Sydney 2000 Olympics. Notably, this statistic excludes live viewings, pubs, stadiums and parties where the game was displayed.

PERFORMANCE RECORD

1	Sydney FC	1st (four times)
2	Brisbane Roar	1st (three times)
3	Canberra United	1st (three times)
4	Melbourne City	1st (twice)
5	Melbourne Victory	
6	Perth Glory	1st
7	Newcastle Jets	2nd
8	Central Coast Mariners	2nd
9	Western Sydney Wanderers	
10	Adelaide United	3rd
11	Wellington Phoenix	

WOMEN'S FOOTBALL LEAGUE

Some clubs are owned by their state soccer associations, including Adelaide United and Newcastle Jets.

For the 2017–18 season a minimum salary was introduced at A$10,000. The average salary therefore rose from A$15,500 to A$17,400. A salary cap was set at A$300,000.

The total salary floor, or minimum salary spend, for the 2020-21 season rose to A$294,000, growing to A$315,000 in the 2021-22 season, with a salary cap of A$450,000, as part of a five-year deal that will see the salary floor rise to A$390,000 by 2025-26. The deal also included improved standards in training venues, travel and accommodation, high performance staffing, and attention to player workloads. The A-League Women minimum annual wage in 2021 was A$17,055.

PLAYER PROFILE

KYRA COONEY-CROSS

Kyra Cooney-Cross was born on February 15, 2002.

In Herston, Queensland, Cooney-Cross began her football journey at a young age, often playing alongside older girls and boys. At 13, she joined FFV NTC and, a year later, successfully trialed for the Mini Matildas.

In September 2023, Arsenal announced the signing of Cooney-Cross.

Her international journey includes being part of the Australia U-17s in the 2017 AFC U-16 Women's Championship qualifiers. She was also named in the Australia U-20 squad for the 2019 AFC U-19 Women's Championship.

Cooney-Cross played a significant role in the Matildas' journey, being selected for the team that qualified for the Tokyo 2020 Olympics and featuring prominently in the Australian squad at the 2023 FIFA Women's World Cup. She played for the Matildas in the 2024 Paris Olympics.

AUSTRALIAN WORLD CUP AND OLYMPIC RECORDS

<table>
<tr><th colspan="9">FIFA WOMEN'S WORLD CUP RECORD</th></tr>
<tr><th>Year</th><th>Result</th><th>Position</th><th>Pld</th><th>W</th><th>D</th><th>L</th><th>GF</th><th>GA</th></tr>
<tr><td>1991</td><td colspan="8">Did not qualify</td></tr>
<tr><td>1995</td><td rowspan="3">Group stage</td><td>12th</td><td>3</td><td>0</td><td>0</td><td>3</td><td>3</td><td>13</td></tr>
<tr><td>1999</td><td>11th</td><td>3</td><td>0</td><td>1</td><td>2</td><td>3</td><td>7</td></tr>
<tr><td>2003</td><td>13th</td><td>3</td><td>0</td><td>1</td><td>2</td><td>3</td><td>5</td></tr>
<tr><td>2007</td><td rowspan="3">Quarter-finals</td><td>6th</td><td>4</td><td>1</td><td>2</td><td>1</td><td>9</td><td>7</td></tr>
<tr><td>2011</td><td>8th</td><td>4</td><td>2</td><td>0</td><td>2</td><td>6</td><td>7</td></tr>
<tr><td>2015</td><td>7th</td><td>5</td><td>2</td><td>1</td><td>2</td><td>5</td><td>5</td></tr>
<tr><td>2019</td><td>Round of 16</td><td>9th</td><td>4</td><td>2</td><td>1</td><td>1</td><td>9</td><td>6</td></tr>
<tr><td>2023</td><td>Fourth place</td><td>4th</td><td>7</td><td>3</td><td>1</td><td>3</td><td>10</td><td>8</td></tr>
</table>

<table>
<tr><th colspan="9">SUMMER OLYMPICS RECORD</th></tr>
<tr><th>Year</th><th>Result</th><th>Position</th><th>Pld</th><th>W</th><th>D</th><th>L</th><th>GF</th><th>GA</th></tr>
<tr><td>1996</td><td colspan="8">Did not qualify</td></tr>
<tr><td>2000</td><td>Group stage</td><td>7th</td><td>3</td><td>0</td><td>1</td><td>2</td><td>2</td><td>6</td></tr>
<tr><td>2004</td><td>Quarter-finals</td><td>5th</td><td>4</td><td>1</td><td>1</td><td>2</td><td>3</td><td>4</td></tr>
<tr><td>2008</td><td colspan="8" rowspan="2">Did not qualify</td></tr>
<tr><td>2012</td></tr>
<tr><td>2016</td><td>Quarter-finals</td><td>7th</td><td>4</td><td>1</td><td>2</td><td>1</td><td>8</td><td>5</td></tr>
<tr><td>2020</td><td>Fourth place</td><td>4th</td><td>6</td><td>2</td><td>1</td><td>3</td><td>11</td><td>13</td></tr>
<tr><td>2024</td><td>Group stage</td><td>9th</td><td>3</td><td>1</td><td>0</td><td>2</td><td>7</td><td>11</td></tr>
</table>

GLOSSARY

Australian women's Olympic team the Matildas

A-League Women the premier women's association football league in Australia

attacking zone players in a forward position

basic shooting technique execute the strike using the laces of your shoe, aiming for the middle of the ball

corner kick a kick taken from the corner arc of the soccer pitch

duration of the game soccer games consist of two halves, each lasting 45 minutes

defence defenders typically operate in the defensive half of the pitch. left defence, centre and right defence

exciting skills soccer is frequently referred to as "the beautiful game," yet to play it with grace, one must first master the fundamental skills of the sport

fundamentals in football, the ultimate objective is to win by scoring goals

free kicks awarded to players when there is an infringement made by the opposition

goal kick unimpeded kick taken by the goalkeeper in the match

goalkeeper the only player in the team that can pick up the ball and whose task is to guard the goal

kick off the initial kick taken in the centre of the pitch to start the game

linespeople assistant referees who patrol the perimeters of the pitch during a game

match day when the top player is prepared to step onto the field and give their maximum effort

media Australian matches are shown on online subscription streaming services and free-to-air broadcasts

midfielders players who link the defence players to the attacking players in the middle of the pitch

national teams the Matildas, Australia's senior women's national soccer team, also represent the country

offside rule an important soccer rule that restricts players running ahead of the ball to interfere with the opposing player's attempt to gain possession

the Young Matildas the women's under-20s soccer team of Australia participates in international youth tournaments

the Future Matildas the Future Matildas program was established in 2018 to provide specialised training for some of Australia's most talented 15 to 20-year-old female footballers

red and yellow cards when a player commits a serious offence that merits a caution with a yellow warning card or a red card depending on the infringement

soccer pitch dimensions soccer fields are generally larger than those of other major sports like American Football, but the size of a soccer field can vary based on factors such as the governing body of the league

substitutions team managers or coaches are responsible for initiating substitutions in a soccer match

the throw-in if the ball crosses the sideline due to a player's body or foot contact, the opposing team receives a throw-in at the spot where the ball exited the field

Women's World Cup thirty-two teams played in the 2023 Women's World Cup. Australia and New Zealand were the host nations and Australia finished in fourth place

INDEX